THE BURNIN(

The Burning Perch

LOUIS MACNEICE

faber and faber

First published in 1963
by Faber and Faber Limited
3 Queen Square London WC1N 3AU
This paperback edition published in 2001

Photoset by Wilmaset Ltd, Birkenhead, Wirral
Printed in Italy

A CIP record for this book
is available from the British Library

ISBN 0-571-20759-6

2 4 6 8 10 9 7 5 3 1

TO MARY

Forgive what I give you. Though nightmare and cinders,
The one can be trodden, the other ridden,
We must use what transport we can. Both crunching
Path and bucking dream can take me
Where I shall leave the path and dismount
From the mad-eyed beast and keep my appointment
In green improbable fields with you.

Contents

Soap Suds

This brand of soap has the same smell as once in the big
House he visited when he was eight: the walls of the
bathroom open
To reveal a lawn where a great yellow ball rolls back through
a hoop
To rest at the head of a mallet held in the hands of a child.

And these were the joys of that house: a tower with a
telescope;
Two great faded globes, one of the earth, one of the stars;
A stuffed black dog in the hall; a walled garden with bees;
A rabbit warren; a rockery; a vine under glass; the sea.

To which he has now returned. The day of course is fine
And a grown-up voice cries Play! The mallet slowly swings,
Then crack, a great gong booms from the dog-dark hall and
the ball
Skims forward through the hoop and then through the next
and then

Through hoops where no hoops were and each dissolves in
turn
And the grass has grown head-high and an angry voice cries
Play!
But the ball is lost and the mallet slipped long since from the
hands
Under the running tap that are not the hands of a child.

Déjà Vu

It does not come round in hundreds of thousands of years,
It comes round in the split of a wink, you will be sitting
    exactly
Where you are now and scratching your elbow, the train
Will be passing exactly as now and saying It does not come
    round,
It does not come round, It does not come round, and
    compactly
The wheels will mark time on the rails and the bird in the air
Sit tight in its box and the same bean of coffee be ground
That is now in the mill and I know what you're going to say
For all this has happened before, we both have been through
    the mill,
Through our Magnus Annus, and now could all but call it a
    day
Were it not that scratching your elbow you are too lovely by
    half
So that, whatever the rules we might be supposed to obey,
Our love must extend beyond time because time is itself in
    arrears
So this double vision must pass and past and future unite
And where we were told to kowtow we can snap our fingers
    and laugh
And now, as you watch, I will take this selfsame pencil and
    write:
It does not come round in hundreds of thousands of years.

Round the Corner

Round the corner was always the sea. Our childhood
Tipping the sand from its shoes on return from holiday
Knew there was more where it came from, as there was more
Seaweed to pop and horizon to blink at. Later
Our calf loves yearned for union in solitude somewhere
Round that corner where Xenophon crusted with parasangs
Knew he was home, where Columbus feared he was not,
And the Bible said there would be no more of it. Round
That corner regardless there will be always a realm
Undercutting its banks with repeated pittance of spray,
The only anarchic democracy, where we are all vicarious
Citizens; which we remember as we remember a person
Whose wrists are springs to spring a trap or rock
A cradle; whom we remember when the sand falls out on the
   carpet
Or the exiled shell complains or a wind from round the corner
Carries the smell of wrack or the taste of salt, or a wave
Touched to steel by the moon twists a gimlet in memory.
Round the corner is – sooner or later – the sea.

The Suicide

And this, ladies and gentlemen, whom I am not in fact
Conducting, was his office all those minutes ago,
This man you never heard of. There are the bills
In the intray, the ash in the ashtray, the grey memoranda
   stacked
Against him, the serried ranks of the box-files, the packed
Jury of his unanswered correspondence
Nodding under the paperweight in the breeze
From the window by which he left, and here is the cracked
Receiver that never got mended and here is the jotter
With his last doodle which might be his own digestive tract
Ulcer and all or might be the flowery maze
Through which he had wandered deliciously till he stumbled
Suddenly finally conscious of all he lacked
On a manhole under the hollyhocks. The pencil
Point had obviously broken, yet, when he left this room
By catdrop sleight-of-foot or simple vanishing act,
To those who knew him for all that mess in the street
This man with the shy smile has left behind
Something that was intact.

Perspectives

The further-off people are the smaller. Grandparents,
Homeric heroes and suffering Bantu
Are nothing in size to the tax-collector
Or the dentist breathing fire on one's uvula.

So the stunted commissionaire bulks larger
Than the massive magnate at the turn of the stairs
While the coffin entering by the west door
Screens the chancel and dwarfs the altar.

Yet sometimes for all these rules of perspective
The weak eye zooms, the distant midget
Expands to meet it, far up stage
The kings go towering into the flies;

And down at the end of a queue some infant
Of the year Two Thousand straddles the world
To match the child that was once yourself.
The further-off people are sometimes the larger.

Château Jackson

Where is the Jack that built the house
That housed the folk that tilled the field
That filled the bags that brimmed the mill
That ground the flour that browned the bread
That fed the serfs that scrubbed the floors
That wore the mats that kissed the feet
That bore the bums that raised the heads
That raised the eyes that eyed the glass
That sold the pass that linked the lands
That sink the sands that told the time
That stopped the clock that guards the shelf
That shrines the frame that lacks the face
That mocked the man that sired the Jack
That chanced the arm that bought the farm
That caught the wind that skinned the flocks
That raised the rocks that sunk the ship
That rode the tide that washed the bank
That grew the flowers that brewed the red
That stained the page that drowned the loan
That built the house that Jack built?

Here, to begin with, is the world
That breeds the race that claims the right
That makes the pace that makes the race
That bursts the tape that rings the bell
That drees the weird that scoops the news
That stews the tea that stales the smut
That gluts the guts that loathe the lights
That light the path that probes the maze
That traps the days that dodge the wolf

That haunts the door that bears the box
That gulped the bills that swelled the debt
That bent the back that caused the pain
That warped the mind that steered the feet
That took the road that climbed the hill
That boasts the yew that chills the ground
That grows the grass that chokes the flowers
That brewed the red that decked the bank
That bears the slab that wears the words
That tell the truth that ends the quest:
Where is the Jack that built the house?

Pet Shop

Cold blood or warm, crawling or fluttering
Bric-à-brac, all are here to be bought,
Noisy or silent, python or myna,
Fish with long silk trains like dowagers,
Monkeys lost to thought.

In a small tank tiny enamelled
Green terrapin jostle, in a cage a crowd
Of small birds elbow each other and bicker
While beyond the ferrets, eardrum, eyeball
Find that macaw too loud.

Here behind glass lies a miniature desert,
The sand littered with rumpled gauze
Discarded by snakes like used bandages;
In the next door desert fossilized lizards
Stand in a pose, a pause.

But most of the customers want something comfy –
Rabbit, hamster, potto, puss –
Something to hold on the lap and cuddle
Making believe it will return affection
Like some neutered succubus.

Purr then or chirp, you are here for our pleasure,
Here at the mercy of our whim and purse;
Once there was the wild, now tanks and cages,
But we can offer you a home, a haven,
That might prove even worse.

Flower Show

Marooned by night in a canvas cathedral under bare bulbs
He plods the endless aisles not daring to close an eye
To massed brass bands of flowers; these flowers are not to
    pluck
Which (cream cheese, paper, glass, all manner of textile and
    plastic)
Having long since forgotten, if they ever knew, the sky
Are grown, being forced, uprooted.

Squidlike, phallic or vulvar, hypnotic, idiotic, oleaginous,
Fanged or whaleboned, wattled or balding, brimstone or cold
As trout or seaweed, these blooms, ogling or baneful, all
Keep him in their blind sights; he tries to stare them down
But they are too many, too unreal, their aims are one, the
    controlled
Aim of a firing party.

So bandage his eyes since he paid to come in but somehow
    forgot
To follow the others out – and now there is no way out
Except that his inturned eyes before he falls may show him
Some nettled orchard, tousled hedge, some garden even
Where flowers, whether they boast or insinuate, whisper or
    shout,
Still speak a living language.

In Lieu

Roses with the scent bred out,
In lieu of which is a long name on a label.
Dragonflies reverting to grubs,
Tundra and desert overcrowded,
And in lieu of a high altar
Wafers and wine procured by a coin in a slot.

On the podium in lieu of a man
With fallible hands is ensconced
A metal lobster with built-in tempi;
The deep sea fishermen in lieu of
Battling with tunny and cod
Are signing their contracts for processing plankton.

On roof after roof the prongs
Are baited with faces, in saltpan and brainpan
The savour is lost, in deep
Freeze after freeze in lieu of a joint
Are piled the shrunken heads of the past
And the offals of unborn children.

In lieu therefore of choice
Thy Will be undone just as flowers
Fugues, vows and hopes are undone
While the weather is packaged and the spacemen
In endless orbit and in lieu of a flag
The orator hangs himself from the flagpost.

The Taxis

In the first taxi he was alone tra-la,
No extras on the clock. He tipped ninepence
But the cabby, while he thanked him, looked askance
As though to suggest someone had bummed a ride.

In the second taxi he was alone tra-la
But the clock showed sixpence extra; he tipped according
And the cabby from out of his muffler said: 'Make sure
You have left nothing behind tra-la between you'.

In the third taxi he was alone tra-la
But the tip-up seats were down and there was an extra
Charge of one-and-sixpence and an odd
Scent that reminded him of a trip to Cannes.

As for the fourth taxi, he was alone
Tra-la when he hailed it but the cabby looked
Through him and said: 'I can't tra-la well take
So many people, not to speak of the dog.'

The Grey Ones

Crouched beneath a snowbound sky
Three grey sisters share an eye;
Before they lose it and forget
Ask the way to Never Yet,

Which might be Once Upon a Time,
Golden Age or Perfect Crime,
Kingdom Come or Free for All,
No past, no future and no fall.

Bandied round from face to face
One lonely eye in frozen space
Skewers the perspectives of the mind
Till what you wished you fear to find,

Which might be what your childhood swore
Lay shrined beyond the haunted door
Or might be where your mentor seems
To misdirect you to in dreams.

Every such what and where betwixt
Your fact and fancy stays transfixed
By that one unremitting stare
Which cancels what you never were,

Who might have been a prince of Troy,
A lord of song, a roaring boy,
Or might have been an idiot mild
Who meets his match in every child,

For all which persons lacking proof
The three grey sisters wait aloof;
They chew the cud, they pass the eye
And check the client next to die,

Who might be in some mountain cup
Where climbers meet it struggling up
Or might be in some Eastern town
Where most men take it lying down

Sprawled against the Gates of Doom
Whence all kebabs and cockstands come,
On which stands guard for ever more
A beggar with a flaming sore.

After the Crash

When he came to he knew
Time must have passed because
The asphalt was high with hemlock
Through which he crawled to his crash
Helmet and found it no more
Than his wrinkled hand what it was.

Yet life seemed still going on:
He could hear the signals bounce
Back from the moon and the hens
Fire themselves black in the batteries
And the silence of small blind cats
Debating whether to pounce.

Then he looked up and marked
The gigantic scales in the sky,
The pan on the left dead empty
And the pan on the right dead empty,
And knew in the dead, dead calm
It was too late to die.

Spring Cleaning

The cripple aches in his lost limb,
The old man cries for a dropped dummy,
Dawn comes up with muted strings,
Spring rides high in a bailiff's van.

Blain and dazzle together, together
Magnolia in bloom and holly in berry.
In the writing desk where nothing is written
Lurk latchkeys, counterfoils and lockets.

The stopnetting sags, the molehills rise,
Typewriters ring, opinions wilt,
Towers of pennies for spastic children
Wobble and crash while the tills ring

The Rites of Spring. Over the sticks
High horses crash, under the water
Black fingers pick at the ocean bed,
The whole flat smells of hot cross buns.

Peace and rumours of peace. Mechanical
Brains compute the chances. Jets
Trace on the skies their ads and prayers:
Let someone soon make all things new.

In spruce new wards new mothers shriek,
New vacuum cleaners run amuck,
New deaf incapsulated souls
Gaze out at noisy birds of dawn;

While on a pillar in the sands
A gaunt man scours his plinth and hauls
His empty basket up and cries:
Repent! It is time to round things off.

Another Cold May

With heads like chessmen, bishop or queen,
The tulips tug at their roots and mourn
In inaudible frequencies, the move
Is the wind's, not theirs; fender to fender
The cars will never emerge, not even
Should their owners emerge to claim them, the move
Is time's, not theirs; elbow to elbow
Inside the roadhouse drinks are raised
And downed, and downed, the pawns and drains
Are blocked, are choked, the move is nil,
The lounge is, like the carpark, full,
The tulips also feel the chill
And tilting leeward do no more
Than mimic a bishop's move, the square
Ahead remains ahead, their petals
Will merely fall and choke the drains
Which will be all; this month remains
False animation of failed levitation,
The move is time's, the loss is ours.

The Pale Panther

The sun made a late and lamented
Spring. Yellow teeth tore
The ribs of my roof. The giraffe
Necks of blind lamp posts bent
To lick up turds and print.
Beyond the electric fence
One tiny tractor stalled.

Milkman, milkman, your empties
Are all to collect; do not wait
Till they jive on the steps, you surely
Know about bugs in the sun,
Runways in rut, control
Towers out of touch, and burns
Whose gift is not to cure.

As for you, airman, your empties
Are broken test tubes or shards
Of caddis, it is too soon
To order replacements according
To the state of play since the green
Lies in shadow now and the tractor
Stalled when the sun stopped play.

Réchauffé

The food on the walls of the dark tombs
Awaits the dragoman whose torch
Will warm it when the deep freeze burns
In the highpitched dried-date voice. By turns
These live men filing past inspect
These dead that serve by turns the painted
Food on the walls of the dark.

The hands on the ends of the sun's rays
Are like small paddles or bats to pat
Piedog and priest on the head and give
Pharaoh and land the chance to live,
Yet even the most sun-worshipping king,
Praise though he will, must also dread
The hands on the ends of the sun.

The dams on the breast of the mad Nile
Secure both budget and mind: what once
Could either prove too scarce or full
Stands docile now like a ringed bull
And yet who knows what sudden thrust
In the guts, what gripe in the mind, might burst
The dams on the breast of the mad?

Ravenna

What do I remember of my visit to Ravenna? Firstly,
That I had come from Venice where I had come from Greece
So that my eyes seemed dim and the world flat. Secondly,
That after Tintoretto's illusory depth and light
The mosaics knocked me flat. There they stood. The geese
Had hissed as they pecked the corn from Theodora's groin,
Yet here she stands on the wall of San Vitale, as bright
As life and a long shot taller, self-made empress,
Who patronised the monophysites and the Greens
And could have people impaled. There was also and thirdly
   the long
Lost naval port of Caesar, surviving now in the name
In Classe: the sea today is behind the scenes
Like his Liburnian galleys. What went wrong
With Byzantium as with Rome went slowly, their fame
Sunk in malarial marsh. The flat lands now
Are ruled by a sugar refinery and a church,
Sant' Apollinare in Classe. What do I remember of Ravenna?
A bad smell mixed with glory, and the cold
Eyes that belie the tessellated gold.

Constant

Too many curds on the meat, too many dark cloth caps
On the conveyor belt that twice a day
Spans the Golden Horn, too much history
Tilting, canting, crawling, rotting away,
Subsiding strata where ghosts like faults, like mites,
Reminders of stagnation or collapse,
Emerge into the mist. After Athens
This place seems of the North, a halfway house
To Tomi or Kiev; the visitors' eyes
Play spillikins with minarets, a louse
Lurks in a banned fez, the bubbles rise
From someone drowned in a sack an age ago,
The Fourth Crusade dissolves in loot and rape,
Theologians, eunuchs, tipsters, goldsmiths, grow
Like fungi out of the walls, this game is high,
Caught between Roman and Turk a dream takes shape
And becomes Constant, known to sailor and exile
For its red lamps and raki, while the sky
Red with repeated fires, accidental or designed,
Sags like a tent over riot and ruin and one
Who calmly, having other things in mind,
Bears on his palm the Church of the Holy Wisdom.

October in Bloomsbury

Edwardian pillar boxes wait for Edwardian letters; the
   Museum
Spreads its dead hands wide, a pigeon scores an outer
On a scholarly collar, the menu in the pub says Butter Beans
   Greens, Peas,
Black men and schoolchildren rummage for culture, the
   tutelary spirits are hard to please,
Those epicureans who haunt the lawns, whose amputated
   delicate fingers tingle,
Whose delicate eyelids are dropped for ever not to be pained
   by the great new institutes,
Who sometimes even when out of mind become what we miss
   most,
In the callbox for instance lifting a receiver warm from the ear
   of a ghost.

Now the parking meters picket and pick the Georgian locks
   and invisible
Meters tall as the yellowing trees docket and dock our
   history,
Though Charles James Fox unconcerned in a bath towel sits
   on his arse in Bloomsbury Square
While plane tree leaves flop gently down and lodge in his
   sculptured hair.

New Jerusalem

Bulldoze all memories and sanctuaries: our birthright
Means a new city, vertical, impersonal,
Whose horoscope claimed a straight resurrection
Should Stimulant stand in conjunction with Sleeping Pill.

As for the citizens, what with their cabinets
Of faces and voices, their bags of music,
Their walls of thin ice dividing greynesses,
With numbers and mirrors they defy mortality.

So come up Lazarus: just a spot of make-up
Is all you need and a steel corset
And two glass eyes, we will teach you to touch-type
And give you a police dog to navigate the rush hour.

With all this rebuilding we have found an antidote
To quiet and self-communing: from now on nobody
Strolling the streets need lapse into timelessness
Or ponder the simple unanswerable questions.

Wheels upon wheels never moving, Ezekiel
Finds himself in a canyon of concrete;
Cage upon cage, Daniel goes feeling
From one to the next in search of a carnivore.

But, that Babel may rise, they must first work downward
To subliminate previous and premature foundations.
Bulldozer, dinosaur, pinheaded diplodocus,
Champ up forgotten and long-dry water-pipes.

Charon

The conductor's hands were black with money:
Hold on to your ticket, he said, the inspector's
Mind is black with suspicion, and hold on to
That dissolving map. We moved through London,
We could see the pigeons through the glass but failed
To hear their rumours of wars, we could see
The lost dog barking but never knew
That his bark was as shrill as a cock crowing,
We just jogged on, at each request
Stop there was a crowd of aggressively vacant
Faces, we just jogged on, eternity
Gave itself airs in revolving lights
And then we came to the Thames and all
The bridges were down, the further shore
Was lost in fog, so we asked the conductor
What we should do. He said: Take the ferry
Faute de mieux. We flicked the flashlight
And there was the ferryman just as Virgil
And Dante had seen him. He looked at us coldly
And his eyes were dead and his hands on the oar
Were black with obols and varicose veins
Marbled his calves and he said to us coldly:
If you want to die you will have to pay for it.

The Introduction

They were introduced in a grave glade
And she frightened him because she was young
And thus too late. Crawly crawly
Went the twigs above their heads and beneath
The grass beneath their feet the larvae
Split themselves laughing. Crawly crawly
Went the cloud above the treetops reaching
For a sun that lacked the nerve to set
And he frightened her because he was old
And thus too early. Crawly crawly
Went the string quartet that was tuning up
In the back of the mind. You two should have met
Long since, he said, or else not now.
The string quartet in the back of the mind
Was all tuned up with nowhere to go.
They were introduced in a green grave.

Birthright

When I was born the row began,
I had never asked to be a man;
They never asked if I could ride
But shouted at me 'Come outside!',
Then hauled the rearing beast along
And said: 'Your charger, right or wrong.'
His ears went back and so did I,
I said 'To mount him means to die',
They said 'Of course'; the nightmare neighed
And I felt foolish and afraid.
The sun came up, my feet stuck fast,
The minutes, hours, and years went past,
More chances missed than I could count,
The stable boys cried: 'Time to mount !'
My jaw dropped and I gaped from drouth:
My gift horse looked me in the mouth.

Children's Games

Touch me not forget me not, touch me forget me,
Throw salt over your shoulder when you walk under a
     ladder,
Fly away, Peter, they are waiting in the Vatican,
Come back, Paul, to your Macedonian runaround.

Hop scotch and somersault ring a ring of raspberries.
Who shall we send to fetch her away? Touch wood and turn
     again.
I'm the king of the barbican, come down you dirty charlatan.
When you see a magpie put salt upon her tail.

He knows I know you know catchum
Nigger by his whatnot round and round the launching site.
Boar's tusks and phonies say the bells of Saint Adonis,
Up Guards and Jenkins and all fall down.

The grand old Duke of York is just about to turn about,
Keep your fingers crossed when Tom Tiddler's ground is over
     you,
I'll beat you in a canter say the bells of Atalanta;
Touch me not forget me, touch me forget me not.

Tree Party

Your health, Master Willow. Contrive me a bat
To strike a red ball; apart from that
In the last resort I must hang my harp on you.

Your health, Master Oak. You emblem of strength,
Why must your doings be done at such length?
Beware lest the ironclad ages catch up with you.

Your health, Master Blackthorn. Be live and be quick,
Provide the black priest with a big black stick
That his ignorant flock may go straight for the fear of you.

Your health, Master Palm. If you brew us some toddy
To deliver us out of by means of the body,
We will burn all our bridges and rickshaws in praise of you.

Your health, Master Pine. Though sailing be past
Let you fly your own colours upon your own mast
And rig us a crow's nest to keep a look out from you.

Your health, Master Elm. Of giants arboreal
Poets have found you the most immemorial
And yet the big winds may discover the fault in you.

Your health, Master Hazel. On Halloween
Your nuts are to gather but not to be seen
Are the twittering ghosts that perforce are alive in you.

Your health, Master Holly. Of all the trees
That decorate parlour walls you please
Yet who would have thought you had so much blood in you?

Your health, Master Apple. Your topmost bough
Entices us to come climbing now
For all that old rumour there might be a snake in you.

Your health, Master Redwood. The record is yours
For the girth that astounds, the sap that endures,
But where are the creatures that once came to nest in you?

Your health, Master Banyan, but do not get drunk
Or you may not distinguish your limbs from your trunk
And the sense of Above and Below will be lost on you.

Your health, Master Bo-Tree. If Buddha should come
Yet again, yet again make your branches keep mum
That his words yet again may drop honey by leave of you.

Your health, Master Yew. My bones are few
And I fully admit my rent is due,
But do not be vexed, I will postdate a cheque for you.

Sports Page

Nostalgia, incantation, escape,
Courts and fields of the Ever Young:
On your Marks! En Garde! Scrum Down! Over!
On the ropes, on the ice, breasting the tape,
Our Doppelgänger is bounced and flung
While the ball squats in the air like a spider
Threading the horizon round the goalposts
And we, though never there, give tongue.

Yet our Doppelgänger rides once more
Over the five-barred gates and flames
In metaphors filched from magic and music
With a new witch broom and a rattling score
And the names we read seem more than names,
Potions or amulets, till we remember
The lines of print are always sidelines
And all our games funeral games.

The Habits

When they put him in rompers the habits
Fanned out to close in, they were dressed
In primary colours and each of them
Carried a rattle and a hypodermic;
His parents said it was all for the best.

Next, the barracks of boys: the habits
Slapped him on the back, they were dressed
In pinstripe trousers and carried
A cheque book, a passport, and a sjambok;
The master said it was all for the best.

And then came the women: the habits
Pretended to leave, they were dressed
In bittersweet undertones and carried
A Parthian shaft and an affidavit;
The adgirl said it was all for the best.

Age became middle: the habits
Made themselves at home, they were dressed
In quilted dressing-gowns and carried
A decanter, a siphon, and a tranquilliser;
The computer said it was all for the best.

Then age became real: the habits
Outstayed their welcome, they were dressed
In nothing and carried nothing.
He said: If you won't go, I go.
The Lord God said it was all for the best.

Greyness is All

If black were truly black not grey
It might provide some depth to pray
Against and we could hope that white
Would reach a corresponding height.

But, as it is, we melt and droop
Within the confines of our coop;
The mind stays grey, obtuse, inert,
And grey the feathers in the dirt.

If only some black demon would
Infuse our small grey souls we could
At least attempt to break the wire
That bounds the Gadarene hens' desire.

But, as it is, we needs must wait
Not for some demon but some fate
Contrived by men and never known
Until the final switch is thrown

To black out all the worlds of men
And demons too but even then
Whether that black will not prove grey
No one may wait around to say.

As in Their Time

(i)

They were so mean they could not between them
Leave one tip behind them; the others
Tipped so wildly it made no sense,
When the cold computer gathered the leavings
It broke about even, made no sense.

(ii)

Polyglot, albeit illiterate,
He stood on a crumbling tower of Babel
Cured of heredity, and though
His idol had a brain of clay
He could not read the cuneiform.

(iii)

She believed in love, but was it
Her self or her role believed?
And was it believed and not
Professed or envied? Lastly,
Was it love she believed in?

(iv)

He was the man you thought
And I thought too was me
That never was on land
Or sea but in fact was at home
On both and never was.

(v)

Year by year these old ladies had saved
For the sake of their nieces and decade by decade
For their great-nieces and greater-nephews
Till the inflation left them nothing
To leave to the heirs that were dead before them.

(vi)

He had clowned it through. Being born
For either the heights or the depths
He had bowled his hoop on the level
Arena; the hoop was a wheel
Of fire but he clowned it through.

(vii)

She had her mind on the main
Drain. When it all was over
She could maintain that the point
Was the main but the point was the drain
Was no more on the main than herself.

(viii)

For what it was worth he had to
Make a recurring protest:
Which was at least a gesture
Which was a vindication
Or excuse for what it was worth.

(ix)

He was to be found in directories,
Admiring asides and footnotes,
Flowers by request. When he entered
A room it at once was a morgue
To tip people off he had entered.

(x)

Citizen of an ever-expanding
Universe, burning smokeless fuel,
He had lived among plastic gear so long
When they decided to fingerprint him
He left no fingerprints at all.

(xi)

She was a bundle of statistics, her skin
Creamy with skinfood, *and* she knew the lingo,
So that when she entered the bush she was entirely
Camera-conscious. For all that the cannibals
Ate her one day they had nothing else to do.

(xii)

As a child showed promise. No need to push him,
Everyone said. Then came the drought
And after that, on his twenty-first birthday,
A cloud no bigger than a god's hand
And after that there was no need to push him.

This is the Life

Down the rock chute into the tombs of the kings they grope
    these battling sandalled
Elderly ladies in slacks and a hurry, their red nails clutching at
    hieroglyphics,
Down to the deep peace of the shelter, everything found,
    cuisine and service,
All the small ochred menials and livestock discreetly in
    profile, every convenience
Laid on free so that they may survive in the manner to which
    they are accustomed,
Gracious in granite – this is the life – with their minds made
    up for ever and the black
Sarcophagus made up ready for the night, they can hide their
    heads under the graveclothes
And every day in the dark below the desert will be one of both
    independence and thanksgiving
So they never need worry again as to what may fall out of the
    sky
But whenever they want can have a Pharaoh's portion of
    turkey and pumpkin pie.

Budgie

for Robert MacBryde

The budgerigar is baby blue,
Its mirror is rimmed with baby pink,
Its cage is a stage, its perks are props,
Its eyes black pins in a cushionette,
Its tail a needle on a missing disc,
Its voice a small I Am. Beyond
These wires there might be something different –
Galaxy on galaxy, star on star,
Planet on planet, asteroid on asteroid,
Or even those four far walls of the sitting room –
But for all this small blue bundle could bother
Its beak, there is only itself and the universe,
The small blue universe, so *Let me attitudinize,*
Let me attitudinize, let me attitudinize,
For all the world is a stage is a cage
A hermitage a fashion show a crèche an auditorium
Or possibly a space ship. *Earth, can you hear me?*
Blue for Budgie calling Me for Mirror:
Budgie, can you hear me? The long tail oscillates,
The mirror jerks in the weightless cage:
Budgie, can you see me? The radio telescope
Picks up a quite different signal, the human
Race recedes and dwindles, the giant
Reptiles cackle in their graves, the mountain
Gorillas exchange their final messages,
But the budgerigar was not born for nothing,
He stands at his post on the burning perch –
I twitter Am – and peeps like a television
Actor admiring himself in the monitor.

Memoranda to Horace

(I)

Aere perennius? Dissolving dialects.
Flaccus, why trouble now to be lapidary,
Knowing posterity, let alone unable
To scan or follow you, neither will be able,
Let alone yours, to cope with language,
Being confined to the usual and frozen
Channels, communicants in frozen sperm,
Caught between cosmic and comic radiation,
Against which world we have raised a monument
Weaker and less of note than a mayfly
Or a quick blurb for yesterday's detergent?

Yet (another paragraph) I should correct myself
Though not for myself or my time but for the record:
Fame you no longer presumed on than pontifex
And silent Vestal should continue daily
Climbing the Capitol. Whether that proviso
Has been properly kept seems open to question
Even though a coiffed and silent figure
Has been seen by some on Michelangelo's piazza
With eyes turned down on the past. Yet your image
'More lasting than bronze' will do: for neither
Sulphuric nor other acid can damage,
Let alone destroy, your Aeolian measures
Transmuted to Latin – aere perennius.

(II)

Returned from my far-near country, my erstwhile,
I wonder how much we are defined by negatives,

Who have no more seen the Bandusian
Spring than have you the unreadable Atlantic,

You to whom seraph and gargoyle were meaningless
And I to whom Roman roads are a tedium
    Preferring the boreens of a country
Rome never bothered her ponderous head about.

So what have we, Flaccus, in common? If I never
Boasted a Maecenas, you never summarised
    Life from Rockefeller Centre
And if you never moved in a Christian framework

I never moved in a pagan; for that matter
I no more found Tir na nÓg than you
    The Hesperides, yet vice versa
If you never found Tir na nÓg, then I never

Found the Hesperides. It looks as if both of us
Met in the uniqueness of history a premise
    That keeps us apart yet parallel,
The gap reducible only by language.

It is noisy today as it was when Brutus
Fell on his sword, yet through wars and rumours
    Of wars I would pitch on the offchance
My voice to reach you. Yours had already

Crossed the same gap to the north and future,
Offering no consolation, simply
    Telling me how you had gathered
Your day, a choice it is mine to emulate.

(III)
'Or with the tangles' as one of our own said
And another called it 'intense' but admiringly 'levity',

[39]

This in the Nineteen-Thirties
Had you, Flaccus, been alive and improbably
    Tempted by the Party would as usual
        Have served as a second string.

Yes, Augustus had to arrive in a sealed train
And you had to praise him and even think you meant it
    The way you meant it for Regulus;
Yet we can guess between politics and personal
    Ties what making your expected
        Bow you really preferred,

Slipping away to Lalage. There in the shade
Of an ilex you could forget the triumphal arches
    And the rigged votes; the repetitive
Cicadas endorsed your sleep after lovemaking
    From which deliciously laughing
        She woke and gave you a phrase,

Which you dressed out in nonsense, that old yarn
Of the routed wolf, and yet today in London
    When all the loudspeakers bellow
'Wolf repeat Wolf!' I can find asylum,
    As you did, either in language
        Or laughter or with the tangles.

(iv)

Though elderly poets profess to be inveterate
Dionysians, despising Apollonians,
    I find it, Flaccus, more modest
To attempt, like you, an appetitive decorum.

Contraptions in ear or mouth or vagina,
To you known neither as aid nor indignity,

[40]

Assist yet degrade a generation
For whom quality has long been in pawn to security.

Which you, though they called you a time-serving parasite,
Must understand, though even your period
   Never foresaw such appalling
Stress upon mere irredeemable quantity.

So now, when faced by a too well evacuated
Sanatorium or mildewed junkshop,
   The point is never to recognize
Any preconception: let commonplace be novelty.

Which you, had they called you a legacy hunter,
Would yet have agreed, no matter how the market
   Jittered: the point was to recognize
The unborn face and the nigger in the woodpile.

Both of which gifts, whether non-recognition
Or pre-recognition, can serve us two thousand
   Years after yours as an antidote
To the poison of time and manoeuvre a compromise

With horrible old fellows, glazed and jowly,
Who were the ones we always avoided
   Yet soon to be resembled albeit
Our juniors resemble ourselves in avoidance.

(v)
Flaccus, there are creatures for you over-Gothic
Met only by twilight, who daylong dozing
By night are too wary: to these I am grateful,
To Cocksnook, Lilith and Harum Scarum.

With whom to hobnob is a mortification
Of self-respect, one's precious identity
Filtered away through what one had fancied
Till now were one's fingers, shadows to shadows.

Which yet means relief from the false identity
Assumed in the day and the city, the pompous
Cold stereotype that you in your period
Tried to escape in your Sabine farmhouse.

Which even for you was somewhat to archaize –
Much more then for us for whom Lares, Penates,
And all their kind are nothing but rhetoric,
Funerary urns from the supermarket.

But how strange to think that degenerate goblin
And fetch have outlasted your classics; at twilight
I go to my tryst, the sky was dirty
All day, there is snow to come, there are monsters

To come and corrupt me, it is almost cosy,
The sly paw gripping the lapel, the hurried
Old lag's tip in the lobby: 'Plead guilty
Before they acquit and adopt you'. *Lusisti*

Satis – remember? Likewise but otherwise
To opt out now seems better than capitulate
To the too well-lighted and over-advertised
Idols of the age. Sooner these crepuscular

Blasphemous and bawdy exchanges; and even
A second childhood remembering only
Childhood seems better than a blank posterity,
One's life restricted to standing room only.

Star-Gazer

Forty-two years ago (to me if to no one else
The number is of some interest) it was a brilliant starry night
And the westward train was empty and had no corridors
So darting from side to side I could catch the unwonted sight
Of those almost intolerably bright
Holes, punched in the sky, which excited me partly because
Of their Latin names and partly because I had read in the text-
  books
How very far off they were, it seemed their light
Had left them (some at least) long years before I was.

And this remembering now I mark that what
Light was leaving some of them at least then,
Forty-two years ago, will never arrive
In time for me to catch it, which light when
It does get here may find that there is not
Anyone left alive
To run from side to side in a late night train
Admiring it and adding noughts in vain.

Goodbye to London

Having left the great mean city, I make
Shift to pretend I am finally quit of her
Though that cannot be so long as I work.
    Nevertheless let the petals fall
    Fast from the flower of cities all.

When I first met her to my child's ear
She was an ocean of drums and tumbrils
And in my nostrils horsepiss and petrol.
    Nevertheless let the petals fall
    Fast from the flower of cities all.

Next to my peering teens she was foreign
Names over winking doors, a kaleidoscope
Of wine and ice, of eyes and emeralds.
    Nevertheless let the petals fall
    Fast from the flower of cities all.

Later as a place to live in and love in
I jockeyed her fogs and quoted Johnson:
To be tired of this is to tire of life.
    Nevertheless let the petals fall
    Fast from the flower of cities all.

Then came the headshrinking war, the city
Closed in too, the people were fewer
But closer too, we were back in the womb.
    Nevertheless let the petals fall
    Fast from the flower of cities all.

From which reborn into anticlimax
We endured much litter and apathy hoping
The phoenix would rise, for so they had promised.
  Nevertheless let the petals fall
  Fast from the flower of cities all.

And nobody rose, only some meaningless
Buildings and the people once more were strangers
At home with no one, sibling or friend.
  Which is why now the petals fall
  Fast from the flower of cities all.

Off the Peg

The same tunes hang on pegs in the cloakrooms of the mind
That fitted us ten or twenty or thirty years ago
On occasions of love or grief; tin pan alley or folk
Or Lieder or nursery rhyme, when we open the door we find
The same tunes hanging in wait as when the weather broke
In our veins or the golden bowl in our hands; they show
Frayed edges here and there or loss of nap but like
Chameleons can adapt to whatever sunlight leaks
Or thunderstorms impend or ghosts of long love strike.
Hence when the coffinlike cradle pitched on the breaking
    bough
Reveals once more some fiend or avatar, we reach
For one of those wellworn tunes; be it purgatory or hell
Or paradise even, circumstances allow
This chain of simple notes the power of speech,
Each tune, each cloak, if matched to weather and mood,
    wears well
And off the peg means made to measure now.

Coda

Maybe we knew each other better
When the night was young and unrepeated
And the moon stood still over Jericho.

So much for the past; in the present
There are moments caught between heart-beats
When maybe we know each other better.

But what is that clinking in the darkness?
Maybe we shall know each other better
When the tunnels meet beneath the mountain.